A Joy Filled Room

BRIAN HICKEY

WESTBOW
PRESS®
A DIVISION OF THOMAS NELSON
& ZONDERVAN

WestBow Press books may be ordered through booksellers or by contacting:

WestBow Press
A Division of Thomas Nelson & Zondervan
1663 Liberty Drive
Bloomington, IN 47403
www.westbowpress.com
844-714-3454

ISBN: 978-1-9736-9867-8 (sc)
ISBN: 978-1-9736-9868-5 (e)

Library of Congress Control Number: 2023909434

Print information available on the last page.

WestBow Press rev. date: 6/29/2023

I

A place of peace,
Is needed to go to,
Especially when you are going through,
I cannot see trees,
Because there is smoke,
But I shall see the trees,
For I have hope,
I constantly travel without rest,
I'm able to travel,
Because I blessed,
I dine at a table,
With a fine wine,
As the Kings did,
In Biblical times.

"Welcome"

II

I drink from the cup,
Of my hand,
Holding on to the plow,
Is a part of GOD's plan,
I sit in the proper seat,
And I meet who I'm supposed to meet,
I travel without bound,
And look to what is found,
I receive for I may give,
And I breathe in order to live.

"In Order!"

III

Purposely I walk,

Towards my destination,

I shall get thee,

With few complications,

I am not counting,

So, I have no equations,

But the ONE that walks with me,

Heals my abrasions,

So, listen to me as I speak to you,

Because I walk,

You should be walking too.

"Arriving!"

IV

Come to me,
When I cannot walk,
Speak to me,
When I do not talk,
Hear me out,
As I do not listen,
Look for me,
If I do become missing,
Consider me is the plead,
And just love me,
Is my need.

"Something Simple!"

V

I pray that you are at peace,
And that no one breaks it,
And throughout your journey,
I pray that you make it,
Rejoice for the blessings,
You will receive,
And share with others who are in need,
And for your journey,
This is a good season,
And why this time,
Only GOD know the reason.

"One Admissions!"

VI

Can you go forward,
If someone is holding you back,
Can you build on mud,
That is moist and stacked,
To WHOM do you pray,
In times of lack,
When pressure is applied,
Do you begin to crack,
I'm shoving you,
To pay for unmerited strength,
And it will be granted,
Worry not the length,
The gathering of eyes you will see
And for the task you've finished you have
received some of GOD's Mercy.

"ULTIMATELY Helped!"

VII

You may enter because you have been invited,
Don't be saddened become excited,
Many didn't get on the list,
In which you have made,
You were invited to,
When others would have paid,
Parking is limited so the guests are few,
And when you arrive, they will be glad to see you.

"Take Your Coat Off!"

VIII

I won't quit, because it is hard,
I was chosen,
So, I will walk the yard,
In darkness I won't see perfectly,
But strong is the faith bestowed to me,
The power that has been given,
I never knew,
And if you believe,
Grace and powers will be unto you.

"Strengthening!"

IX

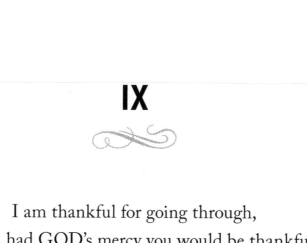

I am thankful for going through,
And if you had GOD's mercy you would be thankful too,
To wake up and see another day,
To speak, and just say hey,
I eat until I want no more,
And my cupboard over runneth on the floor,
And a handful of unsown seed,
Gives me hope beyond which beyond I can see,
As the day end and I receive rest,
Angels are with me for I've been blessed.

"With Me!"

X

I prayed; through the night you kept,
And may you be in peace,
After you've slept,
May your day be bright and fun,
And may your cup overly run,
Tomorrow, may you prosper and receive,
And for the rest of your days,
May you always believe.

"A Blessed House!"

XI

As they watch you rise, they learn what to do,

When you become elevated,

They witnessed that too,

When strength is upon you, you lift.

And spirits smile,

Because of your gifts.

And, because you are a child.

"The Meek!"

XII

Every place you are needed, you attempt to be,
Every place that's in darkness you attempt to see.
Every place that needs a hand,
You attempt to hold,
And every place that speaks of metals you appear as gold.

"Every Place!"

XIII

If you are the Blessed one,
Then you are a tested one,
And I guess one maybe a stressed one,
In the midst of a mess,
Remember the test,
And thank GOD for your trial in a rejoicing confess.

"My Good!"

XIV

I am proud of you,
I love you,
I think so much of you,
I watch you and I see,
A blessing unto me,
Others even push and shove,
In the line to receive your love,
No matter who gets in first,
Your love will even heal the hurt.

"Ouch!"

XV

Please be proud of what you do,
A lot of people depend on your,
A lot of days become at ease,
Because the work you do is aimed to please,
GOD sent someone special for special cases,
A friendly to foreign faces,
An Angel to a host of Saints,
A will to a bunch of aint's.

"Next Day Delivery!"

XVI

Your day is already blessed,
Regardless of attest that you may take,
Just try and do your best,
It will pass time by,
But don't become stressed,
You came to leave and will confess,
Your GOD is the MOST HIGH and never the less.

"Greater!"

XVII

Where will we be when we can't see,
Maybe in a place where we want to flee,
Maybe besides someone who also can't see,
But how would we know if we are not listening,
Prepare for a difference in which you don't know,
Pray to the LORD, so well it will go,
Remember the days you were blessed,
Because there will be days that you are test.

"Final Exam!"

XVIII

Rise, the water said to the tree,
You have strength inside of thee,
You give shad because,
You have fully grown,
And you give life,
More than any has known,
Families sit safely,
Because you provide,
Above many heads,
Are where they hide,
Under you, everything enjoys the breeze,
GOD gives us Grace,
As HE gives us trees.

"And Some Mercy!"

XIX

Nothing was received,
Because nothing was given,
If you want your life to change,
Then, change your living,
If you desire an income,
First come on in,
If you want something to end,
First it must begin,
Ask for the blessings,
You would love to see,
And GOD will begin to show you,
HIS Grace and Mercy.

"A Visual!"

XX

The title to this picture is "Speak Unto!" It shows a pathway which is your journey. But you must complete your journey. And in order to do so you must get on the other side of the mountains. And speaking to your mountains will move them and you will be able to complete your journey.

XXI

Imagine a place,
Where the wind is crisp,
And blows slow,
Imagine a cooling water,
At a calm and constant flow,
Imagine the sun,
Sitting in a sky,
That is a Beautiful blue,
Imagine me on a blanket,
In the park sitting next to you.

"A Picnic!"

XXII

You have pulled for this night to arrive,
For this achievement, you have fought and you've strived,
You have stayed up,
Through the nights,
With papers to write,
Semesters and semesters again,
How did finish?,
Some wonder,
How you didn't take a plunder,
Graduated top of your class with merits and honors.

"Salute!"

XXIII

Grab your staff,

For it is time to walk,

Rest your voice,

Until it is time to talk,

You will speak,

Unto a many faces,

As you arrive,

Unto a many places,

Practice few lines,

For you know not the questions,

As you speak,

Instead of you guessing,

To inform the people,

Is why you came,

And as for the LORD,

bare no shame

"An Assignment!"

XXIV

LORD; Speak to me,
So that I will have direction,
Comfort me,
As YOU make YOUR selection,
Strengthen me,
During this walk of mine,
Allow me to hear,
So I will not speak all the time,
Grant to me,
YOUR Mercy,
As I need it,
And as of YOUR Grace,
Yes FATHER I receive it.

"Promise Keeper!"

XXV

HEAVENLY FATHER;
The Mercy YOU give saves,
And the Grace,
YOU provide allows days,
The shelter YOU have built,
Is more than a roof,
YOUR hands hold us,
Never letting loose,
We chant HALLELUJAH and YOUR Name towards the Sky,
Knowing YOU sit on high,
Remember to comfort,
On the days,
That are dark,
Walking with us,
And never will YOU part.

Printed in the United States
by Baker & Taylor Publisher Services